Out of the Unexpected

Out of the Unexpected
Poems with Sappho

Nichole Turnbloom

WESTBRAE LITERARY GROUP

ISBN: 979-8-9917199-6-4
Published by Westbrae Literary Group
Berkeley, California
Jon-David Hague, Founding Editor

For more information about this and other titles from Westbrae Literary Group, visit us at westbraeliterarygroup.com or email us at info@westbraeliterarygroup.com

*To the mothers
and the daughters before,
and the ones yet to be born*

CONTENTS

3

4

5

Prologue

SAPPHO WAS BORN around 630 BCE on the Greek island of Lesbos. From her nine books of poetry only one poem in its entirety remains. The rest are fragments that have been discovered in the mouths of mummified crocodiles, persons, and even used to heat water when the Romans invaded Greece. An ancient garbage heap in Egypt revealed a treasure trove of her work in the late 1890s inspiring the Victorian poets thereafter.

Sappho's mystery is in part due to the negative space, what remains and what doesn't, that continues to intoxicate her readers and has led to many translations, summations, and even attempts to create "finished" poems. Scholars argue over Sappho's role, position and value, and this often detracts from her tremendous contribution that continues to inspire artists and writers. Sappho played the lyre and sang her poems at celebrations (the origins of lyrical poetry), was a teacher of the arts, a mentor, a mother, daughter, wife, lover and as Plato called her—the 10th muse. Sappho was all of the above. It is in this vein I co-created these poems with her fragments to speak to the parts of our lives that have remained untold, hidden and silenced.

Poets have a long tradition of correspondence through nature, music and art, through words in an epistolary, an epitaph, through various poetic forms, and as a departure from a line as inspiration. This collection is no exception. The poems within contain, depart, and return to Sappho's fragments in a kind of correspondence. Though I read and used multiple translations, the fragments from Anne Carson's *If Not Winter* were like windows that I climbed through and enabled me to experience Sappho as someone I could converse with through time, through the stories and myths that have shaped us, that I wove and unwove to mend, discover, define and redefine myself.

Sappho's work offered me a rearrangement of personal purpose and widening of perspective that I think of as an artistic collision. M. C. Richards might have referred to this as a meeting at the centerpoint. The fragments enabled me to speak to questions, to ponder our political and social ailments, to sit with rage, longing, sorrow, lust and grief that I found difficult to speak of. In this process I was gifted with a perspective that placed me as a witness and conduit, as both and other, that would have otherwise not been possible. When I circled back to edit the poems I found several pieces untouchable because the writing (or arrival of them) was as much of the poem as the words that landed on the page. I wanted to preserve the idea of composition as a particular place and time with or without artistic regret.

I acknowledge with deep gratitude the historians and writers that have preserved Sappho's words and fall in-line with a long tradition of Sapphists. Likewise, I would be remiss without writing that her words stand beautifully in their own light and my additions may in fact detract from them. In such cases, please forgive the liberties taken and simply enjoy Sappho's remnants.

A note on the presentation. All Sappho's fragments are italicized unless the poems are centos (a collage of verses). The fragments were used in the order noted, but not necessarily in their entirety. On occasion a line, phrase or word was extracted as the title, or another fragment was used as a title. The endnotes relate the stories I found inspiring for the poems. The fragment numbers are above the poem titles. The fragments themselves are from *If Not Winter*, by Anne Carson unless otherwise noted. Several fragments are from *Sweetbitter Love* by Willis Barnstone, *Strung with Love* by Aaron Poochigian, and *Sappho* by Mary Barnard and are noted as such. The tile of this manuscript, *Out of the Unexpected* is from a Sappho fragment as well (fragment 16 in Carson). I would be remiss if I did not express my deep gratitude to Carson's translation, without which this collection would have not been possible.

In the unmade light I can see the world

– W.S. Merwin

now thread my voice

– Maya Angelou

Arachne

I have been accused of spinning
  webs over the marble staircase
    in Athens, between the olive grove

and the fence posts on Naxos, across
  the balcony and just below
    the horizon in Aegina. I wanted

to net the sun, to catch the music
  of the muses, as they gathered
    like dew. I wanted to thread

the lost laments of Omphalos, a motif
  that catches, tangles and releases.
    I sought truth as a balm. Prayer

as the language of longing. I wait,
  hidden, listening in darkened
    corners. I have not eaten for days.

87B, 152, and 147

Dear Sappho

My days are spent reading your lines and staring into a mid-place as if my breath had the shape of bone and with each exhale, I could construct the proper connections, I could make myself whole again word by word, line by line. There is a rage I cannot explain, a numbness that accompanies as I try to speak and all I see are bits and pieces, ash and stone. I walk away from your remaining legion spread upon the floor as if separate islands. The pages flutter as canvas sails waving in the wind. They ask for a response, pull at me as if the tide bearing a message to shore.

Dear Sappho,

Yesterday afternoon a gold feathered falcon appeared on the window. I pet the silken head, ran my fingers over the sloped spine. The falcon slept, warmed by the sun. When he awoke, he departed into the misty haze of an autumn fog.

Its presence stirred a roaming *anxiety*, about place and purpose. What is voice when translation is mostly conjecture — the falcon in the mist. The sun's light refracts into a rainbow as Iris carries missives to and fro *mingled with all kinds of colors*, but gold is the hue of the Olympians. Your words bellow such life into me, bend light to unshadow the deep corners I have prayed to neglect. I have no choice but to continue. The *ground*

gives a contentment that you no longer feel. I feel you still as a
nudge to an edge, as a banquet of words shared with the dead.

—yours trully

P. S.

Cassandra,

Do share your divination. There is a value from which there
are no measurements. Though *someone will remember us I say
even in another time.*

Both you and my servant Eros

Nights are always too short where
      we converse (Sappho) in sanguine tones,
      we travel (Eros) with curious eyes
and an occult appetite. I brim with the

nature of being and wake
pensive —
staring at where the
light streaks in.

Watching My Daughters at the Same Event — Ten Years Apart

I used to weave crowns
with delicate white daisies
while sitting on a knoll through
the long days of summer

and later with seed beads
through fishing line as gifts for friends

and later still with raffia braided
I wove baby breath and roses
with lavender and rosemary into
crowns that bloomed with petals scented
to watch as my daughters danced and weaved
with ribbon, over and under, around one another
as they wove bold lines of
blue, purple, red and yellow
into patterns around the Maypole.

I have darned holes
stitched alibis with fingers crossed
interlaced stories with movement,
spun webs into castles,

sometimes out of nothing
with nothing but silence,

and now I am like Penelope
unweaving by the moonlight
under and over, searching for
the lost thread to pull myself through.

A Shovel for My Younger Daughter

She has more flashing fire *about*
her form, more wily wit than *these*
eyes, goose gray, that have lived through *things*
slipped up and down (bruised once again). *I*
manage with humor and sarcastic *groan*
she with flint and much favor. *What*
will history tell of our time; *can*
we untangle the matted threads, sever *I*
and learn to undo to make *do?*

43

At Play the Children War

He teaches strategy in story
tells of the *beautiful he*

reminds of lifting the wounded, the sacrifice
of peace a broken heart can maim.

He speaks of a detour that *stirs up still things*
the guilt bird tweets, *exhausted the mind*

spins its web and *settles*
upon this circle we hold for each

other, *but come O beloved*
we have used our hands as spades

planted our children's garden with
matilija poppies and mountain sages

stumbled alongside our hopes, fed our wicked
bread and water, and are no better or worse.

We have spoken past sunset,
the frog's chorus shimmers in the moon's

beacon low as a whisper on the horizon.
Softly, let us walk for *day is near*.

Mythweaver

> "We have lived our death a thousand times"
>
> — Robert Bly

8

And the children wait unmanifested
    on the horizon of Gaia's inner eye,
    the waterline thick with kohl
    eyes unblinking

    black as the mouth of color before it speaks.
    Sleep as once upon a time, sleep as millions
    of years of evolution in an hour.
    Night only pretends to close its eyes, waits for dawn.

The murder was deep. And death was not what
we thought.

— Clarice Lispector

All Night Long
   after Alejandra Pizarnik

I am aware of the sound of mourning
as the dripping that hollows stone,
a trail that leads to doors
no one opens, *of evil doing,*

of the watchman playing solitaire,
and the keepers of hope dressing
as oracles. The *black sleep of night*
never arrives. Fish beach

without an ocean, birds walk
without trees, bodies arrive
on shores with eyes
that require no translation.

Irises watch the disassembled
gather. Remains of *other*
calm *minds* with ritual
—with something to sing to.

Nightscape

I *dream of black* horses, bronze chariots, shipwrecked.
that *come roaming when sleep* sinking,
conceals me whole.

Sweet god, terribly from pain you ask for lightning,
to hold the strength forsaken.
I hold less. So much less.

But I expect not to share in your glory
nothing of the blessed ones remains. I tend
to your wounds, place poppy seeds at your trembling lips

for I would not like this game of brawn,
toys of iron that clash thunderously, spills
endless fields of rivers red. So red.

But may it happen to me in dream only, the
aftermath dries to dust, lifts like breath
into the morning wind — *all* has happened before.

Love and War

Tender Sister	*Sweet Mother*	Dear Brother
I cannot meter	*I cannot work*	I cannot find
my mind	*the loom*	the way
uncharted	*I am broken*	I am undone
with craving	*with longing*	with anguish
for a god	*for a boy*	for a country
dreamed	*by slender*	once vibrant
in silk	*Aphrodite*	stilled to rubble.

Call Her as Her Name

Ruinous god
        shame would not hold down your eyes
 they became
        piercing breezes
            colored with saffron

I called out
    holding the heart
dawn with arms of roses
        --you burn me
        whiter than an egg

To all on whom the blazing
        makes a way with the mouth
-call her as her name-
        you will remember
        her hair placing the lyre

Eirana the swallow
        innocent no longer
 Memories terribly
            leak
                away.

5

Missing *of the citizens*

Wooded night of inarticulate perfection,
memory lingers as layers of silk
   grieving for the past —

senses no longer feel the gleam of
   millet seeds
as the suns of Helios warming
   the skin through.

Phantoms sulk as they wait
to ask their questions, retreat
towards the sea to rise through
    the mid-light

  once again no
is a river that carries
no remains from where
you once walked,

  but to Kypris
another game and all the winnings
aureate at wrist, the golden
    apple in her palm.

Iphigenia

after Pat Barker

She wears deceit as a
transparent dress
not to betroth Achilles,
but as a father's bribe
for the wind.

The fates unroll her
    last step
        she kneels,
            they cut—
                X (here)

There is no use in crying.
Clytemnestra is already planning
the king's homecoming as the furies
hiss their static rivers into her veins.

Some say Iphigenia
was replaced with a doe,
but the head
slackens just the same.

A sudden breeze is felt
    on the nape
        of every neck.

        They watch, now, for the sails to satisfy.

164

A Thousand Ships

after Natalie Haynes

She summons her son
looks out upon the waves crashing
and the deep ocean, still, in the early light.
It is the contrast that catches: what is
and what once was, and the dwelling on such only
increases the distance shorn. In the sole, a pebble
leaves its rounded impression as a memory crashes:
young and taken in times of war and of a sleeve pulled
taught from behind, still it chokes. Now the skin,
drenched and cooling, burning and shivering
in the salty mist just before dawn. The waves

sigh upon the shore and then swallow back into itself.
Heels sink, sand rises between the toes. Life,
is a fleet of small gifts: the meeting of eyes as a forging
of friendship, the seeds of figs crunching between
the teeth and the sticky nectar of bees. Thousands of years
and still the fig and honey taste just as good. And walnuts
that are said to resemble brains tangles of
perception and thoughts that bewilder, and
the means of cruelty. Then the return, the absence of any

feeling, but pain as another lifetime: the smell
of thyme on her mother, her father's laugh, a small hand
swallowed in her palm. The heart searing a river to the mouth,
and the strain to keep the tide of grief in the opposite

direction. The folding into quarters and then again, so that
the creases are always wrinkles shadowed by loss, a calculation
of long division: an ability to extract some joy in all the
numbers multiplied and subtracted. All the life born
and sacrificed: for the wind, for a promise (broken),
for a slight, for kings and lords and countries and "freedom".

The warriors will not strain to decipher,
(do not ask) their opinion -- on such matters. It is one
of acceptance as a strategic order. A task, a goal and
then the homecoming ("welcome" spells death for some),
and a new generation as half and half.

(They know) mothers will keep on loving, and their backs
are strong and they will carry on and carry on, listen within
the pauses between the sounds of a breath held and released.
The reminiscence of a lingering note of childhood lullabies
before the next score. Of horses unbridled
and the cavernous need of men like a sky that takes
but only reflects minute stars, a shroud-woven of myth
and my hands full of fate that I cannot run from,
and a son that is asked to do the same.

Will my words anchor his humanity
will he remember to look in all directions
will he hold example against the tide
will bravery cease to be anything but
preparation for the inevitable.

of black earth

> One smile the same as the hundred before
with gladness and
> > some indeterminate thing out of place
> > the warriors limp with the unamendable,
> > unpollinated the trees procreate
> > with themselves.
with good luck
> > I will find enough of something
> > to exhaust oblivion. Maybe the rocks move,,
> > maybe a pot can fill, straw brooms
> > will sweep and sweep the dust —
> > so much dust accumulates.

Sailors
> > born of a watery compass with your back
> > to the horizon, have the gods retired
> > humanity, shaken us loose
in a big blasts of wind
> > thrown us off course and shipless
upon dry land
> > burning without water, without billowing
sail
> > to glide across this waving mirage.
the freight
> > is full of tongues parched
> > leeching colors as the threads unravel
> > in the sandy gale waving distractions as patriotic
when

countries fail their people. Time is dice thrown
to the wind, spinning through shreds of decency while

so *many*

skins tan to leather, useless maps brittle
to yellow, clouds with cataracts
stare blankly. Our greatest

works

undress in the night as muses, release
a familiar madness in the silence and

dry land

swells into childhood gardens with
a swing from a tree, a branch of ripe fruit
just as sweet as one remembers.

Bard of Pan

Cave dweller, flutist of the river reeds,
keeper of forest mysteries. I
sing *to tell of* the Amazonians.
I promised a lie, tied the ghosts of Troy
to river stakes and watched as they grappled
spring's current. I fed them bitter roots, not
the herbs where Prometheus' blood dripped.
I slept with their fleshy *tongues* as blankets.
Beneath a layer of sweat, I practiced
memory. In the afternoons I danced
a chorus of lives *to tell tales*
and for a man greater, greater is the
withering. In the end, tongues curled and rolled
fish feasted, and alone I sat with sounds
no bard can sing, no flute can imitate.

Dear Husband,

The air is thick as oil. Orange flames rise in a sunset oozing with flesh. A horse for the gods, for a woman of the gods, another clever trick of Odysseus. Our wall stood impenetrable, our pious pride was not. On the inside, we were defenseless, but *I am not someone who likes to wound rather I have a quiet mind.* I have always been brave, but my fear eats at me, dread consumes me as night falls as a heavy blanket around my throat. Nothing will be left of our home. I will not be able to look upon our daughter come morning and see within her eyes, so much like yours, what she will endure, will become, just to survive.

I want to say something but shame prevents me. I desire to drown our daughter, please forgive me. It is my last right as a mother to give her a resemblance of safety, even as it tortures me. I have watched the men sliced and scared from ten years in battle watching the women huddled in tents, splashing water to wash their feet, their calloused and murderous hands. Women bruised and numb with grief. These soldiers have forgotten they have mothers, grandmothers, sisters, wives, daughters. They line us up in order of youth and beauty-- it is always the same. We persevere while they loot all our names hold-- I refuse to abide.

Elegy of the Iris

Turned inside out the world presses
                    into the night
its stillbirth. Silence will lick
                    the spine of ears, grief

will fill the lake Styx. You must
                    drink its contents
as a liquid scarab rolling its marble
                    sun across all of time

as a drum beat beckons dawn
                    to begin the day
while Charon ferries the souls,
                    listens as a blinded bat

for the sputtering flame of oneness.
                    The great forgetting is a greater
remembering *for when I look at you*
                    stone heavy on my heart, no

longer your voice and laughter,
                    like honey are blowing
through the stone hallways. In the sun
                    I shiver. An ashen rain of frankincense

and myrrh sprouts white irises
                    along the river bank.

Spring Rain

From inside, the night
appears blacker. Light
from three lamps slip
across the streets
of polished doors
reflections catch
at the sill.

why not take off the soft veil
and leave bare all of mortality?

– Francisca Aguirre

Paingiver

The worst givers of pain are silent. A child's yearning towards the shopkeeper's stall catches sour at the throat, smarts the corner of the left eye. Guilt is fondled like an ocean pebble, smooth as skin, and worn away at the center. Your lover leaves for a younger bed. You know what they do, but what do they speak of? The beauty drains from a bouquet on the table, petals darken, twist, and fold as if dancers poised in the last act; to toss them out would admit that it is over, she is not returning. Death passes your window, but doesn't look in your direction.

Sweat

Coruscated on horses after a day's labor. Athletes performing feats of will. Droplets that cascade from drinking cups on August evenings. Knotted concentration collects in droplets on the forehead, descends to stings eyes, while the master watches the apprentice. The moistness that accumulates as I await your lithe feet on the path. Watching him flash his flirt-eyes from across the room and you blush your first-skin. Exertion in song, in love, in play. Phaethon, when he realized the skill needed to chariot the sun exceeded his strength.

Full appeared the moon

Endymion, consort of the night, dilate these pupils with an elixir of the belladonna. Match my longing with your cunning. Medicine my latticed wounds: give Pandora back her jar, Baba Yaga her status, Maria her children's soul, and the dignity of a love that never fades. Give me: a stone cottage in the mountains with an ocean breeze, sandalwood perfume, linen paper to write through the skin to taste the salt of bone. Tonight, the owls hunt silently as the tides rise, as we dance in one circle around no fire. Tonight, we break light like bread and there is always more than enough. Tonight, we swim beneath the temple pillars, walk across the waterline where even the sharpest edge has softened.

Crossable

Determined by: depth of water, strength of current, craft construction, the price of the groping hands of Nessus or coyotes.

Path visibility: as long as one can see several meters ahead this is considered a wise way to proceed. Others would consider this an easy target.

Unpredictable: cross-ability can change and may be a sign from the gods that you are to proceed no further, may not cross at this time through the strait and often narrow. You may prevail, but only after due prayers and a sacrificial promise (your first born).

Consider: a line as "a breathless length" between two places. There is no guarantee that even if breath is held, threshold crossed (as in pain, marriage, career, country) that an office job with a window will provide, a spouse will remain, people will be kind.

To cross anything is to gamble: on chance, on better opportunities, on life or death.

The materials of faith.

The ability to swim in high waters or the ability to find water in treacherous terrain. Note: look for gallon jugs beneath the sage brush.

An infant's head as it crosses through a watery world into an airy one.

Of the springs

In the orchard buds are difficult to see at first, and then they appear bountiful as stars along slender emerald branches. Thousands of promises peek out from budding leaves, like hands revealing a gift. Grasses bright and honorable stand as soldiers, bow deeply, as our feet walk upon their backs.

> Hungry are the offspring for
> nectar, milk, seed:
> chirping, baying, buzzing –
> I grow hungry too
> for your attar lips.

Don't madden my mind

Youth allowed to reap without sowing. Hair tangled in a crown. A condescending tone. An inebriated cackle. Putting words in my mouth and taking out others. Your truth, my silence. Bare ankles. The geometry of love. Hera, when she discovered Zeus had, once again, disappeared.

When did I begin to
substitute
insight for prayer?...

-Frank Bidart

Seven

Fall *moon*
my song *has*
sailed, *set*
across the navy sea, days flake like mica *and*
sisters *Pleiades*
may you cast your net across the *middle*
echo, keep watch through the *night*
to catch what has been lost-- *the*
silver grains gather into *hours*
stagnate into a shallow puddle, it *goes*
black, moves east of mars, then clears, and by and *by*
I hide from my voice *alone*
give until there is nothing less than *I*
bare, staring into a *lie*.

Nepotism

Righteous
>   *with anger*
>>   the grasses riot
>>>   *spreading*
>>>>   obsidian smoke
>   *in chest*
restricted, eyes narrow
to guard
>   what is better left to burn
>   the seethed smile in bitterness
against
no benefit the wise escape to caves,
sip mint tea
>>   *a vaguely*
>>>   disguised retreat to calm a
>>   *barking tongue*
roving in a cage of teeth.

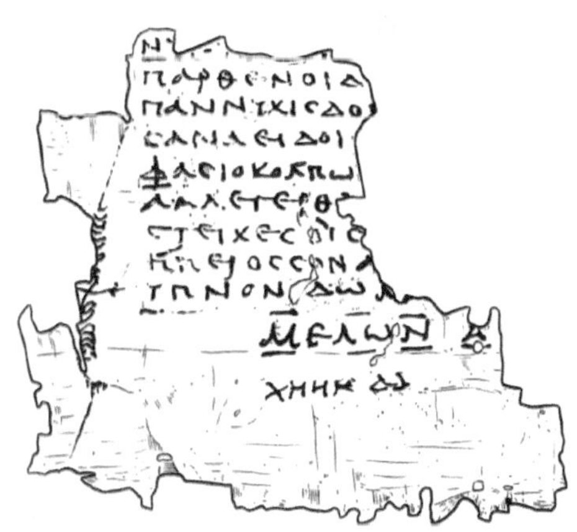
Ν
ΠΑΡΘΕΝΟΙΑ
ΠΑΝΝΙΧΙСΔΟ
СΑΜΑ ΕΗ ΔΟΙ
ΦΑСΙΟ ΚΟ ΚΠΩ
ΛΛΛ СΤΕ Θ
СΤΕΙΧΕС ΘΙΟ
ΚΗ ΕΗΟССΟΝΑ
ΤΠΝΟΝ ΔΩ
ΜΕΛΩΝ
ΧΗΗΚ ΔΙ

Coming of Age

Be nice
>(carry two masks — ensure one is removable,
>skin and neck tone match)

Be quiet
>(scream into your pillow, wipe the spit
>with the back of your hand)

Be beautiful
>(smooth skin with fillers, avoid gluten,
>dairy and sugar--eat air)

Swallow
>(with a chaser of your choice)

Again say
>("yes" and "so sorry" shovel resentment like manure)

Anoint yourself
>(disguise the soft animal within)

Reproach
delicate
Artemis — granted bow and arrow to roam in perpetuity.

Yield
fierce
Athene – Medusa's head displays on your shield

and in her death her spirit
released a white Pegasus.

Are we to wait till then to fly?
I seek…(I seek)
in forked snake tongues
in the turmeric robe of nuns
a language before language.
I sip from the great dipper
drop (by drop) to quench
the thirst of these bodies sacrificed.

I have died still unborn, vanished in
brush strokes, burned myself an island,
sinned and loved, lied and persevered
to truth that stung like a trespassed hive

    either for me
    honey nor the
    honey bee

this is fate's toil, this is my bed
woven of olive and myrtle, wool
and gold. This is where "I" ends and
begin, once again.

Apo 193

> Flesh is a poor investment
> —Nancy Willard

I

But to go there which is both away
and towards
when too   *much*   explanation leads to further rhetoric.
There are two   *talks*   two heads –one demanding, the other serene.
And knowing   much does not grant intelligence of craft,
consciousness   into works of art, wisdom
into heart   of mind
peace in mind.   I want the full recital—
                                  —all else is heresy.

II

It was   *not easy for us*
for those   that have known beauty.
She strayed   inside for months, it gave her ten years
of youth   *to equal the goddess in lovely form*
when ~~eraser~~   already, an alchemy of elixirs,
beads of mercury   herbs and potions, anointing with
rare oil,   treatments by knife,
The holy grail   is a metaphor--doctors of dysmorphia
would have you   pay to believe otherwise.

III

desire   walks through clouds
and   heaven's filament — a breath-promise
Aphrodite   do you live vicariously through the
imperfection   of mortals, pluck their want
with what   was never meant to last.
You give *a nectar poured from*
        flowers that do not grow here
gold   honey (you expected this?)
May I   lick the spout?

IV

Please with   sincerity tell what truth there is
   with hands of persuasion
be-still   the ambitious warrior
towards & away   fighting the death of eye while
monks chant   in heart's resonance to amend avenger —
a right for every   wrong until the last dagger plunges
into the last   bad seed, splits skin
to smoke   spirit from body.

She Calls to Say: It's Cancer.

> To eat one's fill is always a kind of theft
> —Simone Weil

I see our grandfather as Poseidon
with his trident he splits:
the clouds-- they spill
a young girl in her palms
she is holding an Aleutian-blue
      eye of a whale.

He cleaves the moment before
I scream, and sound unformed
become our grandmother's uterus.
He pops the leathery eggs in his
mouth, they squish between
      his teeth. He swallows

Adam's apple, births a seahorse
and *quick as possible*
in a blanket that reads:
      PROPERTY OF ALTA BATES
I run past the riptides where you
almost drowned at five.

I am not afraid to die, my sister
says or maybe it is the seahorse.
The cancer divides as we

speak. The eye blinks. She worries
     after her two sons.

As a child on the long drives
to our grandparents my stomach
tangled into a sailor's net of knots.
I would dream of escaping into
the undulating hills, of spinning
     dry grass into gold.

Our grandfather thunders:
You cannot change the past.
And I remember a definition
of forgiveness as giving up all
     hope for a better history.

I remember the blank pages before us
as a tracing of ghost lines,
the birthing of tongues
that splits open the throat—
     her voice in my hands.

47

Eros shook my mind

Are not my dreams also my biography?
—Olga Ravan

46

Apricot blooms burst
into a perfume piquant
with the possibility
    of our
      convergence.

Hungry (for battle)
I hear the conch shell's
ballad of life
    in love
      with itself.

Dying to live,
falling to awaken
your breath
    moves
      mountains.

I birth my own being.

Mnemosyne

Relentlessly she paces while waiting
for a friend. An imposter in frantic
flight from room to room into her bedroom
she disappears, emerges to confer
at the wide window of an empty porch.
As the light changes, she revises her
garments until night reflects evening black,
lips habit red, pastel face spills into
a puddle too lost to know of itself
or for whom she waits; a mind swept clear with-
out the anchor of memory. Cruel, cruel
fates. *I do not expect to touch heaven.*

 Who can say, in the end, where one came and
 where one goes: mother, daughter, friend or foe.

By Any Other Name
after "Dear Eros"

I have guessed at the work of Eros
Pity my farsightedness

    an arrow I mistook for a falling star
    trembling at the point of flame

        ignited in breast. There is only
        one way to drink *flesh by now old age*

            a hag, a witch, a widow, a mother —
            titles to live by

                (and yet we are
                    so much more?)

        I sleep without repose, stitch
        covers for the unbequeathed

    flies in pursuit of desire left
    to putrefy. Must we, uphold

   noble inclination
   taking no coward as lover —

Sing to us of a history illuminated
by the daily, sing to us of

    the one with violets in her lap
    with hair soft and graying

        scented *mostly* with rosemary.
        The one that *goes astray*, finds strength

          in passion
            & moves
          like water.

Eraser of Leda

In   summer   linen

        a   lilac
shell   hummed
                                                    questions
                                                            hang
                                        in the

                                                            Air
turning   day   to
                                    night.   A
                                        screaming   moth

                                    fell
                                            outside
                a
                    ripple
                                the   egg
                        her   palms
                                    empty

a   brief   Light
                                    a   thousand
            something s   felt

                    at   navel
                                            window   open
                                    her   mouth
                no   sound
                        the bird   flew
                                                            in

2

Downrushing

Three weeks of downpour *and*
roads are impassable, miles to round

a pod of whales deposited *in*
the Laguna, an upturned oak splays

roots reflected in the water as if underground, *it*
silhouettes a white heron as it cuts

the undulating steam as the sun rises, *a*
flock of blackbirds rush upon the water's

surface, barely a ripple. A wheat-colored *horse*
looks worn with the patience of standing

domicile. A mustard *meadow*
shines in contrast to gray remnants

of clouds as they shift over blue, *has*
the season passed so quickly,

may there be more rain to *come?*
How quickly the water overwhelms roots.

How stiff they become in drought, dying *into*
softening, the hill heavy with holding

lupine open their lilac beaks *bloom*
into a gathering at the horizon.

A Collection of Collaborations

But stand to face me, if you are my friend
come flaunt the grace that is in your eyes

      and out of your muteness
      hymns of honeyed affinities.

          Stand face to face with me as a friend
          would: show me the favor of your eyes

      the wolf of longing
      the residue of worship
      the age of stone.
      the rhythm of terror.

          Stand and face me dear; release
          that fineness in your irises –

          wild hooves birth width into
          senses, sound blooms into lilies
          swaying shadows reflect your gaze.

*Sappho fragments are in Italics and are the same fragment
translated by the following: Jim Powell, Aaron Poochigan and Mary
Barnard.

Jacqueline

You only appear *small*.
A lonely lighthouse illuminating
rocky contours, and *many*
heed your warning: change

course, *many*
more like dropped stitches *their*
lives swallowed whole
by the sea. And all you taste
is saline, all you feel
is the wind of *Gorgo*
stinging eyes. And all
I see is light.

94, 174, 24C, and 46

No grove, no dance, no sound

1

She arrived with memories
of forest cathedrals
tasted texture

as a color
between jade
and indigo, tension

as marbles
that crackled
along the *channel*

of spine. Small
enough to disappear
dry enough to ignite

she bent and
swayed to release
an inheritance

as insight to not
incite: anger,
annoyance, a fist…

2

She would *live the opposite:*
swell into creped petals
of a red hibiscus,
vocalize her stake as
a *daring* iridescence

feel a warm
glimmer
trickle
from between her
eyes, into

her belly to
nourish a grove
restore a burbling
creek. A

chickadee
she drank
in head-tilted
sips (too
much at
once
can break
you).

Slowly
limbs lengthened
into melody
to *flow like*
water over soft cushions.

A Translation of Savasana

O wrought, o ponderous woman
starved by sun, cultivated by   hammer.
        In darkened corners
your burdens   grew
and may it rest
        here: heard   seen   held   released.
Your smile restored to its pearly-luster.
O beautiful, o graceful one. May you walk
        in golden rays of self
and find this is your   true   home.

where your eyelashes fell
grow cypress trees
with always at their top
a bird

– Nikos Engonopoulos

4

At the Legion of Honor

Thrice *heart* was stolen by beauty of words alone, and *absolutely* certain it was gone, I demanded its return. "Free will," it claimed. *I can*, against my will, surrender into your coy smile across this garden of sculptures. Sigh, at the bronze arm held at the hip and around the waving tresses between us. Perhaps, I allowed this thievery by telepathy like two swans moving gracefully among reeds while they play their evening soliloquy and you read in French, quoted a German poet. Do you not realize what pulses on your tongue and my neck, so vulnerable. Is it possible I heard my name lift through the blear of dancing glances between statues standing? It *would be for me* far greater to lose all in everything than nothing in hoping so allow your eyes *to shine in answers*, that *face,* those dear lips *having been stained* by blackberries, collected in palm, and fed in bunches one by one.

Middle

You and *I* inhabit words
find where *would* splits like grain
drink the dew *not of genesis but*
rosehips and citrus *think* to recreate
between lines *to* bind lines as
Orpheus with his lyra's *touch*, lead in joy as in sorrow
reflect oceans seven, *the* seven oceans reflect
one striated *sky* that seems so
much rounder *with* you in my
thoughts: *two* great blue herons,
slated wings like *arms* holding up the sky.

40

Secret

But I to you of a white goat
trotting to market for

raisins and almonds while the
children nap I unfold your letters

grow the wings of Icarus,
wait for Zephyr's

quivering to depart, while I
curl toes into an earth too dry

to grasp. I whisper into the
letter's folds:

    Won't you open your gate
    and I will pour wine over

the sun, drink the inked rays
— stain lips unspoken.

Storm of the Sirens

If eyes are doors, then mine are sea caves
and you are my Siren. I suction body
to rock as if a starfish in high tide
as your shadow passes
as a reflection of clouds
– I   dare   not breathe.

A prayer becomes an incantation —
        circling for a place to land
for time to take nothing.

If ears detect the heart's longing
        can you hear the dandelion's
roar through the open wind.

Will the seeds take root where I wish them to?

After the storm I walk the length
        of scents – seaweed sunning, sharp
bay, but it is eucalyptus' seed that I seek:
its crossed navel marks my confession.

Later I remember you
        sipping unfiltered tea
removing the leaves and twigs from
your lips and *with what eyes* did I watch you.

Pheromone

It is (*you, I want*) a mystery you maintain
distraction or eccentricities (*to suffer*) an assay
to distinguish between substance and absence,
a figure of imagination (*in myself I am*) your figure of speech.
A lion waiting (*aware of this*): all must come to the watering hole,
   patience is not a virtue, it is a necessary pawn,
   when one surrenders the throat grows soft--
   the wind carries the scent of Circe.

Reluctant

I wait to stay
a bit longer, nestled
in the turns of your valleys
the ocean of skin,
your neck birdlike
> *(but if you love us)*

this sun that drapes
lightly this room
this tangle of limbs
> *(choose the younger bed)*

a vestige I press into mouth
> *(I cannot bear)*

the distance from limb to limb
a certain death on your eyelids
> *(to live with you when)*

a loose feather falling
> *(I am the older one)*

Violetta

> I shall be like Hebe the cup bearer
> —Voletta in the first act of *La Traviata*

Wealth *nor* youth
one cinches *desire* the
other unleashes
         but all at once

her mouth *blossoms*
into song. There are
consequences
         to a woman's *desire*

wild roses climb:
a wall, a fence,
a garden
         they give

and *take delight*
undetected thorns fester-
draw its
         requiem blood.

Antonym's Sting

I will not count, but
to last all night long
for without her

the maples
torch at sunset
and mute

I can only stare.

Cento

Loosener of Limbs

Sweetbitter unmanageable creature who
steals in. Come here daughter of Zeus.
Never more damaging O Erinna have I encounter you
a child you seemed to me graceless.

I say I have been a strong lover.
You know this, but as soon as possible
you choose the bed of Penthelids.
May you sleep on the breast of your delicate friend.

No longer will I come
bringing to the ends of earth,
to you, handclothes made of flowers,
sweetworded desires wet with dew.

You will remember
no more than a bird with a piecing voice
who looks upon the light of the sun

No longer will I come to you
barefoot, trembling,
to remind you -- knees do not carry
a vine that grows up trees.

Burnout

I have tried now to feel fire
        where none exists; white coals
disappear to the touch and
        I wonder what has burnt out.

What has run its course and must
        now return to dust. I have
given my weight in paper
        made daring by its transparency

when held to the light. I kept stolen
        lines sedged along the
seams. They itch at night, form
        another's skin by imitation.

This does not keep warmth in, but
        rather the tenderest
supple and balmy, but barely
        breathing *my pain drips…*

voice escapes into the evening's
        brightest star watching-in. I
have learned to soften the details
        as if a Monet, jeans that unravel

at their ends, drag dirty along
         the gravel. I know what I want,
but not how to get there, smell
         home as mossy brass, as sweetened

dough with strips of curling lemon,
         golden raisins swelling
in rum, earth's veil revealed in the first
         autumn rain, and dried figs

dusted with crystals
         from its own sugar within.

23

Bird Song

> She can't speak so she paints
> the lines of the pilfered sand-dollar,
> nautilus, lace murex once abundant
> on volcanic beaches, now on display
> in gift shops and on posters
> in museum cafés.

while

> A boy approaches a wise man,
> his hands cupped at his navel
> he asked the wise man:
> "Is the bird I hold
> dead or alive?"

11

> Before she was a bird, she was
> a delicate child, de-flowered and then de-
> tonged. She wove her story as a swallow
> that flies through the stone archways
> abandoned centuries before
> by the Myceneans. Drops hard seeds
> and waste upon certain heads —
> forever is a long time
> to exact revenge, forever is a long time
> without arms or voice.

while

        A child's legs solidify the closer
        the boy grew. Her small mouth released its agony.
        An old woman recongnized that sound, pulled
        the child into a small apartment
        of artifacts. She placed a blanket
        over two caged lovebirds yellow as lemons. Silence
        breathed as the child watched the old woman
        pour tea twice over with mint and chamomile.
        A vase of narcissus between them.

&

    The wise man weights his heart,
    matches eye to eye with the boy,
    and says: "The life of the bird
                is in your hands"

&

        the lone woman smiles at the
        white bells of the narcissus
        rolling off the table. Swears
        she can hear them all ringing
        as the first Sunday after the war.

&

the mute child becomes a nightingale to
announce spring and I know now what I
couldn't say, *you could release me.*

Epilogue

A dream in which Sappho sings "if you have it going on..."

> These poems must be released from their cages
> —Rumi

IN MY DREAM I was standing at a wooden podium at Copperfield's Books. A red pashmina scarf draped around my shoulders, pearl earrings set in a nest of twisted gold, a snake-ring wound around my ring finger. I was reading each poem, freeing the birds that had been trapped in my throat, between my shoulders, caged in the ribs, tangled within my pelvis. One flew from my trembling knees, one from the right wrist as I flipped the page. I was pulling threads apart, opening my flesh as if a weaving, and I had used Sappho's fragments as sweet berries to coax out what was reluctant to fly.

A man in the fourth row hued in tweed bellowed as if from a bullhorn: "How dare you write these poems." My feet softened to wax to seep into the skin of my leather boots. "Blasphemy," his spit sprayed across the heads of the people sitting before him. The books on the surrounding shelves shook in their jackets, dust rose into glittering plumes beneath the fluorescent lights as he glazed over me as if a pot on a cluttered thrift store shelf: worn, base, nameless, worthless.

I began to form a response when from the back corner between philosophy and women's studies walked Sappho. Her hair braided around her head, dressed in a white pantsuit with a lyre in her arms. She began to sing "I am Woman" by Emmy Meli. The audience turned, then stood up as the words from the poems gathered and shaped above our heads as if a cloud of swallows. They landed as three enormous paper-mâché birds with forked feet of gold, and wings the color of the Greek sea. Their bright marigold beaks opened and closed as they sang the backup, waving their wings side to side, shaking their flight tails -- yielding nothing.

The song diffused into every corner of the room. People bobbed their heads and began to dance between the rows of chairs. I watched: bewildered and grateful. Our eyes locked, a smile spread, received and returned from across the divide of chairs draped with discarded scarfs of paisley and worn winter coats. At the last note, she perused the audience and then bowed gracefully. She stepped back and away slowly as the crowd cheered to disappear into the shelves into the resonance of song.

The birds shrank and rose to rest on the brass lamps, on the top of leather chairs, above the book shelves where they preened their sapphire feathers. Calligraphy phrases floated softly as lullaby boats into the folds of people's scarfs, open purses, on the brim of hats, and slipped discreetly into pockets. The birds flew out the twin doors that opened with a yawn to let in the autumn air and a few crunching leaves that somersaulted across the wooden floor. People opened to their own aliveness, spilled into the streets, laughing. Strangers walked arm in arm. The birds flew higher and higher, and higher still.

Who knows where they will land next?

Abbreviations

AC — Sappho. *If Not, Winter: Fragments of Sappho.* Translated by Anne Carson. New York: Vintage Books, 2003.

AP — Sappho. *Stung with Love: Poems and Fragments.* Translated by Aaron Poochigian. London: Penguin Classics, 2009.

DR, AL — Sappho. *Sappho: A New Translation of the Complete Works.* Translated by Diane J. Rayor and André Lardinois. Cambridge: Cambridge University Press, 2014.

JP — Sappho. *The Poetry of Sappho: An Expanded Edition Featuring Newly Discovered Poems.* Translated by Jim Powell. Oxford; New York: Oxford University Press, 2019.

MB — Sappho. *Sappho: A New Translation.* Translated by Mary Barnard. Berkeley: University of California Press, 1958; reprint 1986.

WB — Sappho. *Sweetbitter Love: Poems of Sappho.* Translated by Willis Barnstone. Boston: Shambhala Publications, 2009.

Bibliography

Barker, Pat. *The Silence of the Girls: A Novel*. New York: Anchor, 2019.

David, A. P. *The Dance of the Muses: Choral Theory and Ancient Greek Poetics*. Oxford; New York: Oxford University Press, 2006.

Freeman, Philip. *Searching for Sappho: The Lost Songs and World of the First Woman Poet*. New York; London: W. W. Norton & Company, 2016.

Haynes, Natalie. *A Thousand Ships*. London: Mantle, 2019. (Common paperback: London: Picador, 2020.)

Prins, Yopie. *Victorian Sappho*. Princeton, NJ: Princeton University Press, 1999.

Reynolds, Margaret. *The Sappho Companion*. New York: Palgrave Macmillan, 2002.

Sappho. *If Not, Winter: Fragments of Sappho*. Translated by Anne Carson. New York: Vintage, 2003.

----------. *Stung with Love: Poems and Fragments*. Translated by Aaron Poochigian. London: Penguin Classics, 2009.

----------. *The Complete Poems of Sappho*. Translated by Willis Barnstone. Boston: Shambhala Publications, 2009.

Schwab, Gustav. *Gods and Heroes of Ancient Greece*. Translated by Olga Marx and Ernst Morwitz; introduction by Werner Jaeger. New York: Pantheon Books, 2001.

West, M. L. *Greek Lyric Poetry: The Poems and Fragments of the Greek Iambic, Elegiac, and Melic Poets (Excluding Pindar and Bacchylides) down to 450 B.C.* Oxford; New York: Oxford University Press, 2008.

Endnotes

1

p. 2 Dear Sappho Iris is a messenger of the gods and travels on rainbows. Cassandra (daughter of Priam, King of Troy) refused to sleep with Apollo (sun god). As punishment, he spit in her mouth with a curse that she would be able to see the future, but no one would believe her.

p. 6 A Shovel for My Younger Daughter A golden shovel poem with fragment 58b WB p. 197. Form by Terrance Hayes; inspired by Gwendolyn Brooks.

p. 8 *Mythweaver* This poem is a reverse of a golden shovel poem. Gaia or Gaea—Mother Earth. She united with sun Uranus and created the first people—the twelve Titans (six male/six female). Quote from Robert Bly poem "Ravens Hiding in a Shoe."

2

p. 11 *All Night Long*: Title is from fragment 3 AC p. 9. Inspired by the poem "All Night I Hear the Sound of Sobbing" by Alejandra Pizarnik. La Loba or wolf woman sang over the gathered bones to restore life. White Buffalo woman from the Lakota brought ceremony and scared knowledge to the people. Isis gathered her husband Osiris' remains after his brother Set murdered him.

p. 14 Call Her as Her Name Fragments in order of use: 67A, 137, 61, 71, 92, 60, 86, 58, 38, 167, 65, 58, 44AA, 24A, 103, 135, 68A, 98B.

p. 15 Missing *of the citizens* Fragment 5 AC p. 13. The title is a line of the fragment. Kypris is another name for Aphrodite. The end of the poem refers to the story of the golden apple tree given by Gaia to Hera. Paris must choose the most beautiful woman between Hera, Aphrodite or Athena in exchange for the apple. Each goddess offers a gift (kingdom, beauty, wisdom) if they are chosen. Paris chooses Aphrodite and is promised the love of the most beautiful woman Helen, hence the Trojan war. Aphrodite could be persuaded to assist mortals with fine jewelry.

p. 16 Iphigenia Partially inspired by *Silencing of the Girls* by Pat Barker. In the guise of a marriage to the Achilles, Iphigenia was sacrificed to the goddess Artemis by her father King Agamemnon for the wind needed to sail to Troy. Clytemnestra, her mother, would exact revenge at the end of the war by weaving an armless cape and murdering her spouse. In some accounts Artemis is said to have switched Iphigenia for a doe or another animal and thereafter Iphigenia lived out her days as a priestess.

p. 18 A Thousands Ships Title taken and inspired by *A Thousands Ships* by Natalie Haynes.

p. 22 Bard of Pan Pan is the god of Shepard forests, wild life and fertility. He is part man and part goat and lives in cave. He invented the flute from river reeds, is playful and devious with a keen eye for the river nymphs. I imagined Pan offering respite and refuge for those that ran into the forest.

p. 23 Dear Husband, Letter is from perspective of a mother after the Trojan war when the city of Troy is burning and the remaining women are gathered and distributed as war prizes. Letter was partially inspired by Natalie Hayes and Pat Barker.

p. 24 Elegy of the Iris No Sappho fragment for this poem; it follows the poem before it. Charon is the god that ferries the bodies across the rivers Acheron and Styx, for a fee — the tradition of placing a penny over the eyes of the deceased. If an oath was broken one would be exiled, but if the water of Styx was consumed then exile was postponed for a year. Thetis is said to have dipped Achilles, her son, in the lake Styx to gain immortality. The only part that was not coated in the immortal waters was where she held him, by the Achilles tendon. Paris shoots an arrow that hits the tendon and ends his life. Accounts of Achilles death differ.

3

The shorter prose in this part inspired by the *Pillow Book* by Sei Shōnagon.

p. 31 *Full appeared the moon* Endyiom or Selina is the goddess of the moon. The berries from the Belladonna, one of the deadly nightshades, were used to dilate the pupils in the Victorian era. Dilated pupils were thought attractive and alluring.

p.32 *Crossable* Inspired by *Love, An Index* by Rebecca Lindenberg. Water jugs from article I read in a New Mexico paper about a man that left gallon jugs of water beneath the sage brush all along the border to Mexico.

p. 33. *Of the springs* 103C WB p. 63.

p. 34. *Don't madden my mind* 5b WB.

4

p. 37 Seven Golden Shovel by Terrance Hayes, inspired by Gwendolyn Brooks. Pleiades are a group of stars representative of the seven daughters of Atlas and Pleione. Atlas defied Zeus and as punishment holds the world on his shoulders. His daughters, saddened by their father's burdensome punishment, were placed at his side. In some stories the sisters or maidens are being chased. In other cultural mythologies the star cluster is referred to as the seven sisters, the seven seeds or the seven maidens.

p. 38 Nepotism 158 AC p. 319. In ancient Greek there was a style of poem called a blame poem with a theme of wishing ill will towards someone that betrayed you. This was my take.

p. 40 Coming of Age Some say Medusa was raped by Poseidon and hence turned into a Gorgon whose stare could turn men to stone. Medusa was beheaded by Perseus and displayed on Athena's shield.

p. 42 Apo 193 96 AC p. 193. apo/ἀπό is the Greek preposition that means "from."

p. 44 She Calls to Say: It's Cancer "Forgiveness means giving up all hope for a better past" — Lily Tomlin

p. 46 *Eros shook my mind* Title is fragment 47 AC p. 99.

p. 47 Mnemosyne 52 DR, AL p. 57 Mnemosyne is the goddess of memory.

p. 48 By Any Other Name Inspired by "Dear Eros" by Traci Brimhall.

p. 50 Erasure of Leda 166 AC p. 335 where Carson translates the fragment as:

> they say Leda once found a hyacinth-colored
> egg hidden

I originally wrote a short story of the ancient remains of a society on the island of Santorini, Greece. Similar to Pompei it was buried in volcanic ash but occurred two-thousands years earlier. Instead, the story became an erasure poem.

p. 51 *Downrushing* Title is fragment 183 AC p. 351. Alternate shovel: every other last word, or every last word of the first line of the couplet is from one fragment, fragment 2 AC p. 7.

p. 52 A Collection of Collaborations JP p. 36, AP p. 33, MB p. 71.

p. 53 Jacqueline Gorgo was perhaps a contemporary of Sappho, or one of the three Gorgons, the monstrous winged daughters of Ceto and Phorcys. Stories differ as to why they were turned to monsters. Either they betrayed the gods, or were created to protect Gaia and their faces are used as evil eyes. Medusa was the only mortal one with a human form. The other two share an eye and tooth between them.

5

p. 60 Middle Orpheus was said to sing so beautifully that brooks stopped to listen and beast were tamed. Orpheus played his music through Hades to win his wife back from the dead, on the condition that he could not look at her. At the last moment he did and his wife fell back into Hades.

p. 61 Secret Icarus was the son of Daedalus (a sculpture) who created wings of feathers, cloth and beeswax, to flee King Minos. Icarus (who did not heed his father's advice) flew too close to the sun. The wax melted and wings disintegrated. Icarus plunged to an oceanic death. Zephyr is the god of west wind.

p. 62 Storm of the Sirens The Sirens were three sister, part women, part bird whose haunting songs drove sailors to rocky coasts. Odyssey instructed his men to bind him to the ship's mast and plug their ears with cotton to withstand their haunting song.

p. 63 Pheromone Circe is an enchantress with prolific knowledge of magic, herbs, and potions.

p. 67 *Loosener of Limbs* A cento. Title is fragment 130 in WB. From AC (unless otherwise noted), fragments: 53, 91, 49, 88A, 27, 71, 126, 114, 58, 87F, 101, 94, 73A, 71, 24A, 30, 56 WB, 114, 12, 21, 94, 21, 173.

p. 68 Burnout Fragment 37 WB p. 137.

p. 70 Bird Song In Greek myth, Philomela was raped and her tongue removed by her brother-in-law King Tereus. Philomela weaves the story to her sister Queen Procne who then takes revenge by feeding her son to her father. All three were turned into birds. Philomela a swallow or nightingale depending on the source. Tereus a hoopoe or hawk depending on the source. Procne a swallow or nightingale, depending on the source, to mourn her son. The wise man and the bird story is of unknown origins, though my spouse relayed the story to me after spending three weeks in Wyoming. The third part of the poem is from a childhood memory of an old woman that rescued me from a precarious situation.

82

Acknowledgments

THERE ARE MOMENTS when a decision is made, a book is picked up, a person met, a mentor found that can bring to fruition something that has been waiting for cultivation. I am grateful to have had many such moments and especially for two mentors Judy Halebsky and Paul Hoover from Dominican University's and San Francisco State University's MFA that have shaped the poems within. Thank you to an amazing cohort of poets and writers. Thank you to my family that allowed me to disappear and continued to feed and nourish me in spite of my distraction. It takes a village to raise a child, likewise it takes a village to foster an artist.

Thank you to the following editors that first published these poems.

Bear Review: "Middle" (May 1, 2026)

Luna Luna Magazine: "Eros shook my mind" and "Pheromone" (March/April 2026)

Poet News (Sacramento Poetry Center), February 2026: "All Night Long"

Journal of the Westbrae Literary Group, Issue 2 (Winter 2025): "Watching My Daughters at the Same Event—Ten Years Apart," "Jacqueline," and "Mythweaver"

Write Forward (International Women's Writing Guild Anthology): "Coming of Age"

Thank you, dear reader.